All About Plants

T0080664

All About Leaves

Claire Throp

capstone

© 2015 Heinemann Library
an imprint of Capstone Global Library, LLC
Chicago, Illinois

All rights reserved. No part of this publication may be reproduced or transmitted in any form or by any means, electronic or mechanical, including photocopying, recording, taping, or any information storage and retrieval system, without permission in writing from the publisher.

Edited by Claire Throp and Brynn Baker

Designed by Peggie Carley

Picture research by Ruth Blair

Production by Victoria Fitzgerald

Originated by Capstone Global Library Ltd

Library of Congress Cataloging-in-Publication Data

ISBN 978-1-4846-0507-3 (hardcover)
ISBN 978-1-4846-3847-7 (paperback)
ISBN 978-1-4846-0513-4 (ebook PDF)

Acknowledgments

We would like to thank the following for permission to reproduce photographs: Dreamstime: Egon Zitter, 7, Mommamoon, 16, Erin Packard Photography, 21; iStock: Tedy2g, 12; Shutterstock: Barry Blackburn, 14, Bobkeenan Photography, 17, byggarn.se, 18, Chris Bence, 20, DenisNata, 9, 23 (middle), Elena Elisseeva, 4, Filipe B. Varela, 5, Nataliya Hora, 10, Pefkos, cover, Photobac, 22, pixelman, 13, 23 (bottom), Smileus, 6, 11, Songquan Deng, back cover, 19, 23 (top), Suphatthra China, 15, Triff, 8

We would like to thank Michael Bright for his invaluable help in the preparation of this book.

Every effort has been made to contact copyright holders of material reproduced in this book. Any omissions will be rectified in subsequent printings if notice is given to the publisher.

Printed in the United States 5829

Contents

What Are Plants? 4
What Do Plants Need to Grow? . . 6
What Are Leaves? 8
Types of Leaves 12
Colors. 16
Leaves as Food 20
Plants Need Leaves. 22
Picture Glossary. 23
Index 24
Notes for Parents and Teachers . . 24

What Are Plants?

Plants are living things.

Plants have many parts.

What Do Plants Need to Grow?

Plants need sunlight and air to grow.

Plants need water to grow.

What Are Leaves?

A leaf is one part of a plant.

Leaves grow from a plant's **stem**.

Leaves make food for the plant.

Leaves use sunlight to make the food.

Types of Leaves

There are different types of leaves.
Some leaves are long and thin.

Some leaves have **wavy** edges.

Some plants have very big leaves.

Some plants have very small leaves.

Colors

Most leaves are green.

Some leaves stay green all year.

Some leaves turn red in the fall.

Other leaves turn yellow, orange, or brown in the fall.

Leaves as Food

Some animals like to eat leaves.

Some insects like to eat leaves too.

Plants Need Leaves

Leaves make food to help a plant grow.

Picture Glossary

fall season when leaves turn red, yellow, orange, and brown

stem strong part of a plant that holds up the leaves

wavy many curves in a line

Index

air 6
animals 20
colors 16, 17, 18, 19
fall 18, 19
flowers 5
food 10, 11, 20, 21, 22
insects 21
roots 5
seeds 5
stems 5, 9
sunlight 6, 11
water 7

Notes for Parents and Teachers

Before Reading

Gather together a variety of leaves or photos of leaves. If it is not fall, find photos of leaves before and after they have changed color. Ask children why they think some leaves change color and some do not. Talk about how some leaves change during different seasons.

After Reading

- Ask children why leaves are so important for plants. (They make food.)
- If possible, take children outside and see if they can find a selection of different shaped leaves. Then use books or the internet to figure out the type of plants or trees.
- Work with children to capture ideas about leaves, such as descriptions of their colors, why leaves are useful, and so on. Have them use vivid adjectives and precise verbs, such as *scarlet shapes against the limbs* or *food and shelter for other living things.* After children have contributed phrases, work as a class to combine those phrases to create a poem. Children may add illustrations or photos to the class poem.